DARKNESS TO LIGHT

HOW TO LEARN ENTREPRENEURSHIP FROM A RETIRED DRUG DEALER

BY
MIKE KIETT

Copyright © 2018 Mike Kiett
Edited by: Mike Kiett
Book Layout by Angel Eyes Publications
Cover Designer: Silk Harlan

ISBN-13: 978-1987744125
ISBN-10: 1987744128

MIKE KIETT

PREFACE

Every book, movie, play, speech, sermon or song ever written was done so with an emotional intention or message in mind. In other words, writers want to inform, educate, inspire or motivate. The real goal is a call-to-action. The "Call-to-action" is sometimes for a simple change of thought, heart or behavior. In addition to the intent or goal, the message is delivered in a signature style. Sometimes the writer will personify the spirit of authority, humility, arrogance, and entertainer or as an encouraging life-coach.

This book encompasses all the above. Serving more as a coach, this author shares only a tip of the iceberg of his life experiences and lessons learned, that have traversed him from "Darkness to Light." While some scripts are created and written based on fantasies or wildest dreams, this book is real-life, although some of the scenarios seem unbelievable. The topic is so common that many readers will immediately find themselves or others they know who have or are still treading a peculiar path, or as some call it, the journey of life.

It is the author's hope that the reader will recognize the "Call-to-action," and will do just that... act, for a positive change of thought, heart or behavior, and experience the transition from "Darkness to Light."

INTRODUCTION

Let's be clear! Writing this book is not to glorify or justify the selling of drugs. Drug dealing is a heinous act against mankind-whether it's sold on a corner of a city street; in the home of a suburban town or when sold legally as medication by corporate America. These acts of commerce should never be committed. And while it may bring prosperity to some, it has a domino effect that leads to poverty; depression; distrust; slavery; abandonment; loss of values and death of a person and of a community.

At the same time, I'm not judging. I understand the power that it possesses; the false sense of hope that it offers and the illusion of a better life that it paints. I know what it's like to feel hopeless, hungry, desperate, lonely, optionless. The need to survive and the want to escape this life only fuels greed, desire and desperation. Leaving, in the eyes of many, only one answer, one savior; Drugs. Even still! We are human beings.

As human beings, we should never sacrifice the life of another human to enhance our own lives. This consideration is for drugs, love, deception, theft and more. The one thing that separates humans from animals is the fact that we don't need to kill each other to survive. We have the capacity to make decisions that stem from compassion, love, joy, respect and admiration for one another. It is our responsibility to always put these values first.

I understand all of this because I was once a part of this sub-culture. I allowed "The game," as it is referred, to control my actions, compromise my values, and in a way, take over my mind. Blinded by the desires to be involved and produce the greatest results; no attention was paid to the process.

At the time, I couldn't see that my talents, dreams and values were being pushed aside, all so that my ego could take center stage. Once you allow that, once your vision is seen through the eyes of your ego, then your defeated. And the only way to regain your win, is to die. To die before your dead, is to kill your ego.

~Eckhart Tolle

The purpose of this manuscript is to show how things that are done "In the dark," eventually, can lead to the light. You see, darkness doesn't really exist. Darkness is just lack of light. It took a lot of heartache, failures, and many mistakes for me to figure this out. In these upcoming chapters, I am going to share with you, stories of my life that happened in the dark, but was secretly the blueprint to creating my light. In a conversation-like style, I loosely use the pronoun "You," to share stories that held powerful lessons, underlining values and concrete strategies that are useful for building a business mindset and a successful business.

DISCLAIMER

Now, I can't guarantee this book will make you a million dollars, because I haven't reached that yet. Becoming a millionaire is a mindset. It is the same strategies as anything else but with larger sacrifices. To achieve a million dollars, you must first learn to make 100k and before that 10k; I can guarantee you these strategies will get you there. So, as your coach, at least for this book, if you want to learn the rules and the strategies of the game- to make money, turn the page.

Story One

South Philadelphia was a rough stop. To live here could be compared to living in your own world, on your own planet separated from the rest of Philadelphia. Growing up in "Da P", which it was nicknamed, you were sure to be left with permanent scars, some physical, some emotional. Your journey would start with you attending the neighborhood school, which was mostly ran like a prison. Metal detectors, security guards, police officers, more emphasis was put on enforcing order then education.

The only requirements to be accepted in the school was to have a heartbeat and an address within that school zone. To pass to the next grade, you just had to know how to write your name for attendance; enjoy going to summer school for all the days you missed, and have a mother that would curse the teachers out anytime they tried to give you a letter grade of an F.

The neighborhood bodega, which is grocery store in Spanish, played as your market, sports gambling ring, drug stash spot and if you were really dug in, your hide out from the police.

Everyone male that worked there was named Papi and every woman named Mami. We couldn't pronounce their real names because they also were in Spanish, so that's how we referred to them and how they referred to us.

The Chinese restaurant was your night of luxury dinning; especially, if you could get chicken wings, shrimp fried rice and a shrimp roll with some extra duck sauce; you might as well have died that day because heaven couldn't be any better.

Before your school days, your first daycare was run out of an open dope house. The teachers or babysitters was an old man named "Unc," who wore the same blue velour sweat suit with open toe sandals every day, and a booster; Someone who stole clothes and resold them at half the price, whose name was something like: Tameesha, Sacouya, or Lee, or some other name that just had way too many vowels in it.

Your brother was probably your cousin too; and your mom's husband was named "Uncle Buck," because he either used to be your father's best friend or he really is your uncle. Sometimes you could not always be so sure. Your grand pop ran an illegal lottery business out of the basement- from the window. And your grand mom sold dinners every weekend to pay bills, pay bail, and to support her drug habit. All your uncles where either just coming home from jail or they were on their way back in. Your aunts where the real entrepreneurs. They braided hair, baby sat, sold weed and hid coke for their drug dealing boyfriends... all from the backroom of a two-bedroom house.

If you were a man growing up in South Philadelphia, there were only a few things that you got recognized or respected. You either sold drugs and made lots of money; you were smooth and had all the girls, or you were the one with the heart; bold enough to do pretty much anything, like fighting any man, or even having the guts to shoot a person. Some men were good enough to have all three. However, just having one of those would win you over the girls.

There were only two exceptions to this rule. One, you were a star athlete. Everyone rally behind your success and hopes you would take them with you to that better life, and some made some money off you by betting in the games. The second exception that could get you recognized or respected was, you could wheelie a dirt bike. For some reason putting that powerful machine up on one wheel and holding it up long as possible sent pride throughout the neighborhood.

Then there was me; I failed every test. I couldn't hoop, fight, talk or ride; plus, I was broke...zero dollars. And with the mother I had, selling drugs was impossible, and being spoiled was out of the picture. The brain I had was my gift, and my ability to write well was my talent, although they didn't mean anything to the people around me, especially to the people on the streets; my gift and talent were like pennies with holes in them...worthless.

I couldn't even really relate to the way other people grew up, especially larger families. I was the only child for most of my childhood and my mother was an only child also. So, in some ways, feeling different was normal. While most of the neighborhood kids attended the local public schools, I went to catholic school- all the way until I graduated from high school. Perfect attendance was a must in my house and coming home with a "C" grade was borderline failing.

Home, for me, was a shelter from the rest of my world. My mother worked different decent jobs, had a college degree, didn't partake in and drug use not even cigarettes, and she was also married to one guy since I was two years old. My step-father was a state prison guard. He was hardworking, a good provider and he too was against anything drug related. They wouldn't even allow family members who did drugs to step foot into our home. My grandfather was an Ex Seal from the United States Military, a ship builder and a retiree from the local school district. My grandmother worked in environmental services for as long as I can remember for different hotels and eventually retired from the Philadelphia International Airport.

In retrospect, given the good character qualities of my family, I was sort of like a walking contradiction around there. But I lived a double life. You see secretly, I was a cold-hearted killer. The most feared man to walk South Philadelphia streets. Every woman wanted to be with me and every man wanted to be me. It's just that once the alarm clock went off, and the sunlight crept through my window blinds and I was forced to open my eyes to a new day, my secret life would disappear.

But this would all soon change. The day that I left for college and arrived on campus, was the last day of the life I formally knew. From that point on life would be different. Up until this day of college, life was basic and structured for me. Now it would be spontaneous, and mysterious and it would become, a journey.

In fact, going to college wasn't even on my to-do list. But affirmative action and a 6'4, 280lb college recruiter named Mr. Jones had different plans in mind. I was drafted; oh, excuse me, I was accepted into

K Town University. It was a small college with about ten thousand students and only about 500 of them were Black. The college sat in a small town surrounded by nothing but farmland and highways. This new landscape, and newfound culture so different from South Philadelphia, was scary for me, wasn't that far from the experience of prison, except for the fact that you could have sex as much as you want.

After a few months into the semester, my stomach started to growl louder than the thoughts in my head; it was time to find work. I applied everywhere, but with the freshman schedule being all over the place, it was hard to find a job around my schedule. The only good thing was that in school you could get this thing called a refund check. The one I received was enough for me to buy a nice first car and do some shopping for about a month. Finally, after searching and searching for a reasonable job, the only place that understood my time restraints was the local pizza shop. I was hired as a pizza delivery guy.

In the beginning, I would do only the deliveries that the other driver couldn't get to. Until one day the driver pulled his last no-call, no-show; and got fired. That provided for me the position of head driver. I was given a permanent route. Most of the people who ordered food were either students who stayed up late nights studying, or some older couples who lived in the college town.

One night, I made a delivery to a fraternity house up on the hill. After ringing the bell a few times, the door was answered by a tall, skinny blue eyed blond kid. He was shirtless but had on pink beach shorts in the middle of October. That was actually pretty normal for me to see. The biggest culture shock of my life, was the two-white guys, standing behind this kid, getting high from marijuana. This might have been normal for most, but for me, it was crazy. Maybe I was naive to this situation, but I saw the scenario as weird, because between the schools I went to and the neighborhood I grew up in, white people were depicted as perfect, drug free, violence free, and problem free.

After a few more pizza deliveries throughout the week, an idea popped into my head; I figured why not just buy some marijuana and start selling it; I would be the only dealer to have the drugs and the munchies. So, I did it.

I did that for a few months. In fact, I didn't even go home for my first semester break, I stayed up school and continued my new career. Everything was going great until one day I walked into work, and my boss asked to speak to me in the office. He immediately let me know that he knew what was going on during my shift. Startled, but no that surprised. It was only a matter of time before someone would catch on to my activities. People were calling the pizza shop asking specifically for the "Black delivery guy" every day.

So, I took in a deep breath and embraced myself for whatever punishment was about to happen. He offered me two options. Option number one was that he would call the police and have me arrested. He assumed I had marijuana in my car at the time...and he was right. Or option number two was that I could voluntarily quit my pizza delivery job and agree to supply him the weed- at the wholesale price. My eyes nearly sprang out of their sockets; with one big word forming over top of my head, "Duh!" "Wow," I said, just that fast I went from being a worker to being the boss.

This was great now; all I had to do was supply him, while he supplied the people that called the shop. In return, I had more free time to chase women and find more clientele to sell to. Then one day he called me to meet him at a party. Parties usually meant "Big-money." So, I called my supplier and doubled up with inventory. When I arrived at the party, I met up with my ex-boss.

The place was full of smoke. That wasn't so impressive. The image of seeing a line of white kids, vacuum eight balls of powder off the mirror that sat on the table, into their nose, was Oscar award winning. Powder was a form of cocaine that people snorted up their nose. First marijuana, now cocaine. Everything I knew about the world before college was now obsolete. All these kids in here chasing a dream of becoming doctors, lawyers and even world leaders, snorting years of education away and all I could wonder was, "If this is how they party in the White House?"

While in the bathroom, I overheard guys in the hallway talking about how much they paid for the stuff they just snorted. Now, I wasn't "A Drug Lord," but I knew that those prices were three times the price in the hood. I looked in the mirror, waived my hand farewell, just as my mother and friends did on the day I left South Philadelphia, bound for college. "Good- by marijuana and hello cocaine," I smiled. The rest of my first school year played out like the movies, as I imitated in my dream.

Focus on relationships, not transactions

"Learn this and you will never be broke."

Jan 2005

Into a New Year, I had been home for a few weeks because of the semester break. This bought me the opportunity to check in with a few of my friends before I went back to college. I linked up and drove around for a few days and nights with my friends Slim and Bundles. They were partners on the same crack phone; and they made money together. Crack is a form of cocaine that is cooked with baking soda and water, which enhances its effects, and is then smoked in a pipe.

Slim, well obviously was skinny. He was about six feet, either a little under or a little over. He had a scar from a dirt bike accident that travelled from the top of his head to the top of his left eye brow. He wore a chip tooth from a fight he was in as a teenager, four against one, and he came out on top. That's why he refused to fix it. It was his reminder to others, that despite his weight, he was tougher than the average man. He would work the morning shift and Bundles would work the night.

When they first told me the shifts they worked I thought Bundles working the night shift was a play on his skin complexion. It was too good of a coincidence that the guy who was nicknamed midnight, would be working during midnight. To make matters worse he wore a beard that covered his face from his mustache to the middle of his neck. It was like putting black gloss on top of black paint. He was no were near 6 feet. Maybe and I might be pushing it, 5'6. Didn't have any noticeable scars that I knew about, but his hair was enough. He was going bald by 18 years old and refused to just cut it off. Somehow having enough hair to brush in the middle of his head made him feel better about himself.

They had two totally different personalities and approaches to life and business. For instance, while Bundles was friendlier, more laid-back and personable.

Slim was more, as one might call, snobbish. He was cold hearted and strictly business. He treated the customers like customers; it was all about the transaction. In other words, all he wanted to know was how much money they had for him, and what they wanted. He didn't give deals; didn't do any credit and didn't want to small talk. In fact, he wouldn't even allow the customers to touch him. He used to carry a bottle of hand sanitizer. And every time he exchanged money and product with them, he would use it right in front of them. He had no compassion.

I preferred spending my time with Slim, because he was the one who sipped lean and got all the girls. Lean was a cough syrup medicine with promethazine and codeine in it. You sipped and drank it to get high. I like the taste and even enjoyed the high occasionally. It mellowed you out. While Bundles was usually "Wifed up," or in some committed monogamous relationship and smoked marijuana all day long.

Marijuana was good, but it stank. Each time we were pulled over it would just give the cops a reason to pull us out the car and search us.

One night, I just couldn't sleep; so, I called Bundles to come get me, so I could ride around with him. When he came inside the house to pick me up, he was already smiling. As always, his eyes were half closed and dimmed; the results of some good weed. We snapped fingers, and he started his usual ritual with calling me: "Bow Wow," a nick name I received when I used to wear braids. This name never got old for him.

A few moments later, we were in the car reminiscing about the old days, keep in mind, we were only 18 years old. Suddenly, the phone rang, and Bundles answered: "Yo baby; awe man; I miss you too sweetie, you need me? I'll be right there. Who's that in the background, Timmy? Ok, no problem, 'Ima' stop by 'Micky D's.'"

He hung up the phone and drove off right after he lit up another blunt; and we finished our conversation as usual. We stopped by McDonald's; Bundles ordered some food, and then he drove over to his girl's house; I assumed. We pulled up the block, and instantly I realized we were in the good part of the city. In this part of the city, Black people aren't even allowed to pass through, let alone own homes. I swung my body towards his, "Ayo Bundles, 'my man,' are you cheating with a Becky (white girl)?" I threw my head back and howled with laughter. I continued to tease him. "Yo, I never thought you would ever cheat- especially with a white girl; 'you da man Bundles, you da man!'"

Bundles gave me a real puzzled look. My harassing and interrogating continued. "What, don't tell me your girl got that much money and pull that she lives back here?" As soon as my rhetoric sprang from my mouth, the back-door opened. In jumped Jenny. I knew her name because I had just seen her earlier with Slim. "Thank you Bundles; you're a sweetheart," Jenny managed to say, with a half-smoked Newport in between her lips. Then with fingers in a scissor form, she removed the cigarette, and leaned over and kissed Bundles on the cheek, with her bluish, pink, crusty lips. Bundles did the transaction with her and then handed her the bag of McDonald's food. The moment she got out the car, I faced Bundles to interrogate him even more after I witnessed what had just happened. "Bro., what are you doing?" "What!" Bundles Shouted. "I don't believe you; I added. Food and a kiss, she's a fein (drug addict)" His eyes drilled right into mines for a moment. He pulled another drag on his blunt, rolled the window out to toss out the roach (small piece of blunt), then let the smoke out in my face. He explained to me that I had the wrong attitude.

He preached that when we are out here selling drugs, we are not the only ones out here selling drugs. Feins like buying from dealers whom they like. "They are people just like us; they got kids; family; religion; morals, and feelings. I treat them as friends. Why do you think they keep calling?" Bundles pressed on: "Ayo, if you want to be remembered by them, and if you want them to put your number first on their list, they gotta love you. Especially if you don't want them to rat on you. **Listen to me when I tell you this, cause this best thing I'm ever going put you D with!**" He turned his head to me, executed a smile as always; and he continued to drive. I sat motionless, and listened to him answer every call with, "Yo baby; hey buddy; where you been, and so on."

That following Monday, I went back to school and changed my whole mindset. The last semester was special; it was my first time in the "Game", fist time I ever sold drugs. But, from that semester on, I was determined to become the ultimate dealer. The first step was to now introduce myself as Zack. A name like Zack sounded friendlier, cooler and more Caucasian than my other alias, Reem.

No longer was I going to play the mute at parties. To achieve my goal, I would have to become sociable. In fact, that was a must. That meant slap hands, chest bump, pull fingers, even a wedgie or two if needed.

Even greet guys with friendly words or phrases like: "Yo dude, or hey big guy." I participated in as many beer pong games that I could handle. I went so far as to dress like them- the college kids… all to fit in and somehow brand myself. I became more involved in class activities because they respected intelligence a lot more than the circle I normally entertained. That year, Zack became a household name, not just in the drug business, but in the important social circles as well.

Flip that.

Focus on relationships not transactions. Be more in tuned with your customers. Become your customers. Engage in conversations, ask about their day. Find out their birthday or even make sure you correctly pronounce their name. Business does not run on money as most would say. Business, is ran by people. It is fueled and energized by individuals with their own worries, personalities, dreams, fears and lives. The key to a business, a relationship, a career, is selling yourself, before your product.

For example, most people would rather shop from their local bodega or mom and pop store if the workers and owners refer to them by their name. Or imagine getting your hair styled or cut from a stylist or barber who never talks to you. That would be extremely uncomfortable and detrimental for their business. Even as far as education. When you pick a school to go to, they don't just beat you in the head with statistics and education talk. They introduce you to all activities and community services because that is the personality of the school.

Supply and Distribution

"Without supply and distribution fundamentals, business can't even exist"

Summer 2005

I remember when I first got the idea to sell powder in the city; it was during my first summer break from college; and I didn't realize how hard it would be for me to make money in the summers; it was a nightmare. I made all my money in college during the active semesters, and by the time school break came, I was broke. Didn't quite figure out how to make money in the city, so getting ahead in terms of money, felt like I was spitting in the wind.

The potential customers I met were broke. The product quality wasn't that good, and the amount of police always circling the corners made it hard to even try to make money. I spent most of the summer sitting on the corner, wasting time. I sometimes waited for hours for someone to walk up and purchase a drug or two from me. I was moved to a point where I would have been happy if I sold a "nick" bag just his style, first-hand. He pulled up in a brand new, cherry- red Marauder. This was the elite vehicle to have. In 2005, this was considered the best- for a car style. He jumped out of the car, wearing a pair of jean shorts, tennis shoes and a white tee shirt.

The chain he wore around his neck glistened in the summer sun, and the diamonds in his watch danced around like a dollar party in the winter time. Although he was casually dressed, he looked smart, classy, and like a million dollars. It puzzled me because he used to be known for being dirty. And he was for sure stupid. Suddenly, I became a little jealous - not because he was getting money, but because I couldn't figure out how he was beating me in the game. I mean, I looked better; thought better, and talked better. Having seen how he turned out had me doing some serious self-analyzing. It was time for me to do some research.

The steps that lead to the entrance to a house in the ghetto, were equivalent to a couch in a therapists' office. Here took place, countless conversations, much needed venting, and even a few tears were shed, all in efforts to understand behavior, and remedy a problem. In the neighborhood, some of the older persons-usually men, served as seasoned life coaches. They were referred to as an "Old head." Unlike the office- based licensed therapist, these older men offered more coaching and less counseling. They operated from real-life "been there, done that" experiences- in contrast to the licensed therapists who tend to operate more from book-based theories.

The steps that were always open to me; never needed to make an appointment, and never had to pay a fee, was the ones belonging to an ole head "Akmed". Akmed was almost 60 years old but didn't look a day over 45. He often sat outside on his steps to watch us young guys move throughout the streets. He said it made him feel young again. Akmed had a traditional Philly appearance. He wore a long, thick beard, with streaks of red dye throughout it. The henna dye disguised spots of his natural grey hair. His complexion was deep brown; but his eyes were hazel, which was rare because it was usually the light skinned guys who had colored eyes. After many years of fast living, ripping and running, he was burnt out. At one point in time, he used to be "big time" and well-known in the streets until he got arrested, indicted and sentenced to 120 months in federal prison. When he came out, he used whatever money that the police didn't take and bought his home and started a car mechanic business- a few blocks from his house. Even though he had changed his ways, his mentality and his movements still resembled the kind of a guy that represented the street life. Occasionally he would slip up and say a few slang words that were popular in his day.

We talked every day. He would tell me, I was the only one out there who could hold an intelligent conversation, and that's why he gave me his time. Now, after seeing Rameek's apparent success, I was anxious to find out what the hell I was doing wrong. So, I sat on the steps and started to plead my case to brother Akmed. Once the last word dropped from my lips, he stared at the ground for a few seconds, and then chuckled, then the questions started to roar. "First off youngan (young man), is your product good? Is your weight good? Is your price good?"

My ears were hurting from straining to hear him; he always talked in a raspy whisper. Once the words connected with my brain, I replied in order: "I buy the same product that everyone else out here buys; it's the same size as everybody's dimes are, no smaller. In fact, maybe even a little bigger, and I charge ten dollars, but take all shorts." His facial expression showed is irritation with my answers. That's when the sessions began, "Well, that's your problem youngan. You are exactly like every other jive turkey out here. In this game, there is plenty of competition. Just because you have a drug or product, that don't mean the people gonna buy from you. How about getting better product, doubling up on your bags or offering half off?" He added.

After that lesson, he might as well have grown an extra head or two more eyes. Either way his words were just as crazy and unbelievable. "If I do that, I won't make any money." He leaned closer to me and calmly uttered, "Then you shouldn't be selling what you're selling. If you can't be different, then you lost already; if you want to continue selling it, you need to find it for better and cheaper. **Now this is the most important jewel anybody ever going drop on you!**" His response echoed through my brain. I let his words manifest for a few moments and before I could respond, he spoke: "As far as Rameek, yeah well he is stupid ya know. But you are only as good as your connect (supplier); whoever he deals with never runs out and has a great product. It doesn't matter how smart you are, good is good and cheaper is cheaper, ya know."

Later that day Akmed introduced me to one of his old buddies. Two Russian guys. I didn't even know Philadelphia had Russians. They didn't talk that well, but they counted better than anyone I ever met. They sold me the product with a 30% price cut and 60% more potency. That next morning, I was selling my dimes for five dollars, with the exact same size, but half the price. After that session with Dr. Akmed, my summer went great. No more hungry days, and a few exceptional nights with random females and liquor blackouts.

Flip That

There were a few key points in that lesson. Lesson number one was that, if you don't have a competitive advantage, then you should not be in that field of business. It is very rare that you are the only one in a given field with your product. Customers are bombarded by salespeople and advertisements all day long. You must bring something different or better to the table. If you have nothing to offer with a competitive advantage, then drop that business and move on because you are doomed and will fail.

For e.g. Let's take McDonald's and Burger King. McDonald's is the number one fast food burger place in the United Sates and right behind it is Burger King. McDonald's was known for having the best fries and a good burger. Burger King decided to focus on their burgers. Unlike McDonald's burgers, Burger King's burgers are flame broiled. This is their competitive advantage. If they would have come out trying to make the same burger and fries as McDonald's, they would have never been successful.

Lesson number two was, you are only as good as your supplier. With business, if you sell a product, then your supplier must be consistent. Your supplier must sell to you at a price that allows you to make a generous profit and give you room to price-cut and offer deals when necessary. Also, they should consistently supply you with a decent quality product.

You will be able to stay in the game – if your supplier sticks to this requirement; and you make sure you have enough suppliers where you never run out of product, and you never should pay too much, and your quality product must be consistently good.

Hiding Money

"This rule is essential to building your wealth. A lot of people can gain wealth, but only a few can hold on to it. Remember, you don't save money for rainy days; you save it so that you can invest it later."

Summer 2006

The second year of college was a blur. The lessons and connections I received from Akmed over the summer, carried me into my sophomore year. This was the reason behind this absence of time. All my memories involved drugs, beer and Advil. When reality started to come back into focus for me, an entire year had passed, and it was summer all over again.

This summer went a lot better than my previous summer. I was doing well for myself- selling about $500 dollars a day in product, which equaled to $300 a day in profit. Now this wasn't extremely noticeable in this game, but I held my head above water. I worked for about only 8 hours a day, since it wasn't my operation and I was only a worker for the summertime.

At the end of every night, I would take the money out of my pocket, and rubber band it into amounts of $250, and then put them in my drawer. The next day, my mornings would start with zero dollars in my pocket, so it would be easily noticeable how much I brought in for the day.

Now, the kicker is that every time I wanted to buy something, mostly clothes or food, or to go out on dates, because I was only 19 years old at the time, I would just take money out of the drawer and pay for it. My mentor "Chill" would always try to drill in my head that my first $5000 dollars didn't belong to me; it was security. The first $5000 was for bail or a lawyer- just in case I was arrested. I tried to stick to this.

Like I mentioned earlier I like to shop. The sun was blazing this summer afternoon that was my excuse for a fresh lay (new outfit). I drove down South Street. South Street was Philadelphia's Rodeo Drive. It was our shopping, food, Jewry and social strip. I double parked on South Street, in a tow away zone in front of Dr. Denim-a clothing store. The plan was to run in, grab a few polo t-shirts, and run right back out.

Now these stores are loaded with young women who are pretty, and wear clothing a few sizes too small. Their whole objective is to flirt with the male customers, stroke their ego in hopes to entice them to spend all their money in the store. In most cases it worked. When I walked in, I was fresh bait. What was supposed to be a five-minute trip turned into a half an hour process, all because I wanted to show my money off.

In the middle of a conversation with one of the sales girls, large beeping noises could be heard from outside the store. The moment my ears noticed it, my heart felt it. Yeah, you guessed right; my car was being towed. I was sick.

My initial reaction was to try to bribe the tow truck driver to take the car off the flat bed; but it didn't work. He just gave me the phone number and address to where they were taking it. Now, if you ever had to deal with PPA, you know how dragged-out this process could be. While down at the tow yard, I finally get called up to the counter and the lady told me I owed $2200 in parking tickets. My jaw dropped to the floor.

I hailed a cab back to the house, ran up the stairs and went into the drawer- only to realize that all the dipping in and out of the stash (savings) left me close to broke. There were only three rolls left, totaling $750. Add that to the $200 in my pocket, brought it to a grand total of $950. The moment of truth weighed in heavily; it was time to borrow some money and there was only one person I could call: "Chill." Once the call was made and the story was explained, he agreed to let me borrow what I needed, but not without a little criticism. The only thing he was concerned about was why I didn't have enough money saved?

So, I explained the process: $250 a roll- tucked away in my drawer. He interrupted me in mid explanation, "That's where you messed up kid." I thought he was talking about the rolls, maybe they should be $500 instead. He continued, "You should have been putting money in your mattress, and not in your drawer." I retorted, "Why does it matter; drawer, mattress, shoe box?" He told me, "Cut one end of the mattress, stand it up, and drop some money down there, and hit me back kid." After doing what he said, I got it. It was a lot more work to try to get that money out. Once the roll fell somewhere in the middle of the mattress- in between all the springs, there was no way I would keep going in the house to get that out- just to spend it on pointless objects. **That was the most important lesson I ever learned.** The only problem then, was that was my only $750 I dropped in there. I had to rip the mattress open, and call "Chill" to borrow some more money for a new one. What a day!

Flip That:

This a great strategy in protecting your wealth. If you are an entrepreneur, self-employed or a business man, and want to build and protect your wealth, put your money in places that can't be touched so easily. Open separate bank accounts with only savings accounts and no debit card. If you have a cash business, open a safe deposit box and put money in there. The best idea is to drive to your nearest county or bordering state, open a savings account with their local credit union or bank and store your money there, because you know you won't take that ride every day to spend petty money. Protect your money. Hide your money from yourself.

Play Broke

"Playing broke is probably the hardest rule to get. Living below your means is a concept that is difficult for the unsuccessful to understand. This one method could be the fuel that keeps your drive going!!"

Fall 2006

The first week of my junior year, I thought maybe it would feel different, but it felt exactly like every other semester. I continued my same routine… went to class and saw what my schedule was like and called up some old clientele to see if they were still at the school this year. Linked up with one of my closest buddies, "Lefty" to figure out how we can have a better year. We always came up with the same answer: get more money!

Towards the end of the first semester- around Thanksgiving break, Lefty and I were sitting on my living room floor smoking a blunt. We talked and reminiscence about our college adventure. The conversation brought me to realize that our college years were almost over. After this year, we would have only one more year left to graduate; and then we would be released into the real world.

Once the high kicked in, and my brain wheels went into over- drive, I started preaching about what I think we needed to start doing to be prepared for that day. The gist of the sermon was investing our money into real estate and using the proceeds from that to create a business.

"We can't just keep getting high, getting dressed and getting laid!" I proclaimed Lefty. His response, in between coughs, was "Why not?" I wasn't surprised, you see, Lefty came from nothing. He had a broken home, no family, and no real friends. This right here was life. He probably was trying to think of a way that we could get another four years out of this place.

The more I smoked, the more I vented. Eventually admitting Lefty that I never seen $10,000. Now, I used my little savings trick up until that point, and it worked; but the money didn't come in fast enough. I counted my money from out of my mattress right in front of Lefty, and then counted my product. I had $4300 in cash and $1400 in product. While taking inventory, I swayed my head left and right; let out a big sigh and reached out for the blunt one more time. Lefty coughed horrendously and blurted out, "You got too much money Cuzzo."

This comment took me over the edge. I just spent the last 4 hours talking about how we need more money, and how I never reached 5 digits, and he came up with that stupid response. In an angry rant, I screamed, "Have you listened to anything I said man? It's like I talk for my health!" He looked me dead in my eyes, unfazed by this childish rant, then simplified it for me "I've been listening to you whining, but you ain't listening to me. You got too much money; if you put all that useless money into your cop up (inventory), and continue to do it, eventually you'll have $10,000 or more. Why do you need money sitting? It serves no purpose. Buy more drugs, and you'll have more money. Then he snatched the blunt out of my mouth, that was resting wide open after that reality check; and he smoked the rest of it. He just made perfect sense. He chimed in one more time "Cuzzo." I looked up as he exhaled the last little bit of smoke, then continued **"I should charge you. That's the best piece of advice you ever going get."**

I tried his theory out really hoping that it didn't work so I could throw it back in his face. But by time February of that following semester came, I surpassed my goal of $10,000 and reached $13,700. I would have kept rising but unfortunately, life took another route and I spent all that money on legal fees. Next chapter in my life...

Flip That:

Obviously, the moral of this story is to play broke. Having money sitting around doesn't do anything for your business or your future. Some savings are good but until you reach that nest egg that you really want, the best thing you could do is to put all the money back into the business. Buy more products, hire more people, invest more into marketing, because investing money is better than saving money, especially if you are just reinvesting back into a business that you created. Also, human beings are known to work better out of necessity. They work harder and perform better with their back to the wall. When starting a company just reinvest every single dollar back into your cop, so to speak, after all expenses are paid.

E.g. If you sell t-shirts buy more t-shirts. Buy a better t-shirt printing machine. Then hire an artist to come up with better artwork to put on your t-shirts. Hire a social media marketing company to put you in front of a larger platform.

March 2007

I got arrested spring 2007, on the college campus for possession of a firearm without a license. It destroyed my chances of law school, my reputation with my family and especially my confidence. This incident resulted from- by far, the worst decision I made in my life. Now, what in the world was I doing with a firearm on a college campus? Was I trying to be a gangster; was I terrified of someone in school; was I going to be the first black mass school shooter; none of the above." Let me briefly explain this story.

That semester I happen to make more money than ever. When my hunger for a fancier car became larger, I decided to feed it. Now, I already had a candy red painted grand marquise; it had 24" rims, very clean and attractive. Going into my senior year, I wanted to be a little more adult, and a little more sophisticated. The right kind of car could give me that feeling. There was no better car in my price range that could achieve that but a Cadillac.

Before I bought a new car, I was going to sell my old one and put the balance to it. Now, I had someone ready to buy this car, but they hated the rims; I had to sell them separately. The moment I posted them, some guy that had the exact car but, in a money, green color, reached out to buy them.

When we met up, the buyer didn't have the whole thousand dollars for them. He had $500 cash and a firearm worth $500. Now I first refused the deal; there was no need for a firearm. But after discussing it with Slim, I was eventually swayed, and accepted the gun for half of the payment. Now, I never used the firearm, and never even carried it on me. It collected dust; it sat in the cushions of my couch until one drastic day.

Home for the weekend and bored out of my mind, I rented a car just for the thrill of driving a new car, and the attention it would bring. The goal was to get a few drinks, attend a few parties and see how many girls I could pick up while fraudin (pretending) for the weekend. Saturday morning, I staggered into my home having stayed the night out. My grandmother stood in the middle of my living room, as I walked in. The house I lived in was mine, but it was one of those family houses, passed on from generation to generation. My grandmother lived across the street. She had the keys and whenever she was in the cleaning mood she would come across the street and clean my house.

That day she decided to focus more on the living room area for some deep cleaning. While she swept and mopped the dining room, in arms reach, of the couch, so dangerously close, I was nervous and worried she would find the firearm in the cushions. I complained to her that the steps need a good sweep. This made her changed directions of her cleaning process and head towards the steps. When she climbed up the step to begin sweeping them, I grabbed the gun, and tucked it in my pants before she returned down the steps. Once she realized they were already cleaned from the day before, she looked at me suspiciously and told me to get out her way, so she could finish. I kissed her on the head and walked out. I strolled to my car, opened the trunk and stuffed the firearm into a bag.

Now, I finished the rest of my weekend in the rental car until it was time to give it back. Once I took it back on a Sunday, I was going to stay the night, and leave early Monday morning. But I received a call from my friend, who went to the same school. He was arguing with his mom and his girl, and wanted to go back that night; so, we did. I rolled up a few joints, jumped in my car and smoked and drove all the way there. Once I got to the campus, I was pulled over by campus police.

The smell of smoke escaped from my window once it was rolled down. There excuse for pulling me over was speeding; 10mph in a 5mph zone. Once the officer smelled the smoke that was his leverage against me to forget that he just racially profiled me to pull me over. Knowing that I was wrong at the time I ignored that fact. He made a deal with me. That if I let them search the car and if they found nothing; they wouldn't charge me a DUI, so, I agreed. That's when it all went downhill.

Once the officer made his way to the trunk of the car to conduct the search, there it was: the gun. I was arrested on the spot. They were so excited. This was the biggest bust of their career. It was bad timing too, because just two weeks earlier, there was a shooting at some real popular school down south. It was kind of Ironic; I was so afraid of my grandmother finding out about my gun, that I got caught by the police instead. It never pays to be sneaky. Even though this was a tragic story, it turned out to be one of the most educational experiences of my life. Well, not the actual arrest, but the domino effect afterwards.

Test Drive

"Test Drive" is the easiest solution to building clientele, yet the hardest for entrepreneurs to apply."

May 2008

After about 5 months of trial over that firearm in school, I had to serve 10 months in prison. Not too much time because it was my first offense. When I got out, all the nightmare stories were true. Couldn't go right back to college because financial aid was no longer available, and no one would hire me because of my record. The house bills were backed up, and even the cocaine business was doing badly, both aspects. The prices were way too high, and all of it was stepped on or cut. After a few months of trying and trying to get a job or do something positive, I gave up. It was time to get back in the game, but this would be the first time I had to depend on making money in the streets of Philadelphia. Times before were just something to hold me over until I got back to my school operation.

I washed a few cars; and cleaned out some basements and saved up about $75. This was about half of what was needed to buy the lowest product available. While contemplating how I was going to scrape by with this $75, and not spend what had been saved so far, Slim called me. He asked me to ride with him to get something to eat at the Liberty Place. I agreed to go; even though I knew I wasn't spending any money on food. One hundred and fifty dollars to get 3.5 grams of cocaine was the only objective on my mind. It's what was needed to get this business started.

Now the Liberty Place was this big building where on the first floor there were popular retail stores. The top floors included offices, high-priced condos, and a popular food court. Slim picked me up, and we headed over to, Liberty Place, most of the time driving in silence. When we got there, we headed straight for the food court on the second floor. We walked to this cheesesteak spot that Slim wanted to eat from; we were stopped by an Asian guy who offered us a piece of chicken on a toothpick. He was giving them out as free samples; I took one and tasted it.

Slim turned to me and asked, "Was it good AHK?" And then he started laughing. My face must have told it all. We stood in line at the steak place and finally got called to the front. He asked me what I was having to eat. My response caught him off guard. "Nothing, I only got $75. I'm trying to save up for an 8 ball (3.5 grams)." Slim looked around, lowered his voice then leaned into my ear; "You gotta chill AHK!" He continued, "I got you; go head get what you want to eat. After this, we goin slide to my crib. You goin help me bag up, and Ima give you a lil 8 ball to help you get on your feet." I darted back to the Asian spot where I got that chicken on a pic and got the largest platter they had with extra chicken.

When we were finished eating, we left the Liberty Place and headed to his house. Now when we got in the living room of his house, there was this long table with a scale sitting in the middle, a box of blue baggies size 34, which were the biggest, and a box of red baggies size 12x12 skinnies', which were the smallest.

Slim slid me a plate with about 21 grams of crack cocaine on it, all together in one rock. He handed me a razor and some gloves and told me to bag up as many 12x12 skinnies' as I could. We put Young Jeezy's album on while we worked. Close to the end of the project, I glanced over to see his work, and seen how big his rocks were. They had to be $20 because they looked just like shark teeth. That left me to assume my rocks were either $10 or even $5 bags, if I compared them to his size bags. My curiosity got the best of me, so I broke the silence. "Slim. Why you selling twenties and nicks? Why not just stick to the twenties?" He replied as he always did "You gotta chill AHK! What you're putting together is samples. I'm handing all them jawns (replacement for any noun) out!"

Hearing that made my skin crawl. "I'm over here struggling to get by and you about to hand out almost $1500 worth of drugs for free?" "Why are you wasting all this?" His head spun around to face me, "AHK, this ain't wasting; it's business. This is going to get my phone popping. This is going to get me more feins. How you expect people to buy from you and they don't know how it is?" "Yeah", I added, sarcastically, "but they are crackheads. Tell them you got crack and they're going to buy it." He shook his head in a yes manner, "You're right, but if they know mine is butter (good), then they most defiantly going to cop (buy) off me." A sigh of disbelief escaped my mouth and my eyes Ping-Pong to the top of my head. Once he saw me in doubt, "Oh, so you ain't a believer huh AHK? Well, I'll give you an example. What did you eat at the Liberty Place today?" I replied, "Chicken from the Asians; why?" "Why did you buy it?" He retorted while smiling at me moving his hand in a circle indicating me to hurry up and answer. "Because I was hungry" would have been the obvious answer. But I chose not to respond so fast.

Suddenly, I got it. The image of me taking that piece of chicken from that toothpick and shoving it into my mouth played over and repeatedly! I just sat back and smiled. Once again, another whack at my ignorance. When I looked over at slim who was admiring me contemplating. He just uttered **"Ahk. Don't ever say I ain't teach you nothing. Best lesson in drugenomics you ever going hear."**

I knew at that point how I was going to start my business off. He let me give him $75, and in return he gave me 7 grams of crack cocaine. I put together all 20 bags, but took out 3 grams as samples, and began to pass them out. Before the night was over, I got my first sale. It took me two or three flips to be profitable. After continuously following this method; it was all worth it.

Flip That:

Now you don't have to give samples to start a business, but it is one heck of a boost. Think about it, would you see a movie if you never seen the trailer? Would you buy a car if you never test drove it? Would you rent a house if you never seen the inside? The key to this is simple: people are more likely to buy if they know exactly what they are getting. Think about it, do you remember when magazines or post cards came in the mail, with the one page where cologne was sprayed on it? That was a sample. If multimillion dollar companies use this method. Who are we to not to oblige. There is also a second marketing behind this. Customer perception **(your**

reputation). By giving away free products, you build brand loyalty **(loyal feins)** because you come off trustworthy. You also look as if you are a prosperous business **(getting money)**. If you have it to give, then you have it to sell.

This was my most important lesson!!!!

Hard Work

"Hard work is a very basic concept; it is the most difficult concept for some people to adopt. But it is the cornerstone for all successful people"

June 2008

Thirty days into my new business venture, the traffic started to plateau. The same amount of money was coming in daily, which was a good thing, but there was no progress. Slim's advice of the samples had worked, but I was running out of people to give them to, and even the people who liked the stuff only called here and there. I got a business call from Dot one day to meet her at her home.

Dot was this fifty-year-old white lady who had been getting high for a long time. She was popular amongst all the dealers and could be a pain in the ass because she always wanted something for free. She was blonde with brown eyes, and always answered the door in a white house coat. Whenever she called, it was exciting because, "Pain in the ass, maybe she was, but she was a gold mine." Almost every user in the city came to her house to get high or called her to see who had the best product out.

She rarely called, but it just- so-happened that I was out late one night, about 3 a.m., after going to this club. I was drunk as hell, answered the phone- just to be funny, but it was her. Right away, I sobered up. She only called for one bag, that didn't matter; this was my time to try to "lock her in" **(woo her)** for future business. Now when I pulled up and went into the house, I went right into salesman mode. Starting off by asking "why she doesn't call me. What did I have to do to get her business?" Then pitched to her, that I was the fastest on deliveries, my product was always grade A, and she could get any deal she wanted. After her constant dismissing my plea, with "I got you babe; don't worry about it," she walked me to the door. Right before I went down the steps she grabbed my arm and explained "The reason why I don't call is because you close too early. I called you once before around this time and you didn't answer."

"I have to sleep sometimes, Dot; I pleaded, I go to sleep early so that I can wake up early and be ready." Her response was everything. She schooled me, "In this game sweetie, you have to be on call 24 hours. There might not be a lot of business during these hours, but if you answer everybody's calls now when our usual dealers are not around, you will get everybody's daytime business too."

I never went to sleep on the job again. Well okay, I did, but I made sure that I never slept hard enough to miss a call. I would take naps throughout the day- sometimes even on the floor with books as a pillow. Most of the time I just slept in the car with the phone tucked in the side of my hat, right next to my ear, so when the phone rang I could hear everything. This was before headphones was popular. In just 20 days, I more than doubled my cash flow. I went from making $850 a day to $1800. This just boosted my enthusiasm.

Flip That.

Business is war. It doesn't matter if you're in sales, service or entertainment. To win you must out- beat everyone. You must work hard and be willing to commit sweat and tears for your business. The most important thing is finding out what your competition is slacking in. If it's availability, then you fill that gap. Grit equals great! For example, when the average McDonald's switched to staying open 24 hours a day from closing at 10pm, they increased profits by hundreds of thousands of dollars a year.

Rewards and Gaming

August 2008

Things were going great. Money came in faster than ever before. But $2000 a day in sales equaled $900 in profit. Once shorts, credit, and expenses were subtracted, it turned out to be more like $600. That still wasn't bad, but I wanted more. The only way to get more profits was to sell more drugs. To sell more drugs, I needed more feins.

Maximizing my time was important to pull this off. Every time I wasn't going to a transaction I would ride around looking for more people. Eventually, you run out of people and places to visit. Then most of the people who walk the streets are the people you don't want to deal with. They scavengers. Once winter time hits, and the street walkers no longer walk the streets, this strategy is going to have no return. I would call people and beg them to introduce me to more people, or at least show me more people. They always promised that they would, but never did.

It was time for a break, a day to myself. When I woke in the morning, I got dressed and went to New York. My voyage ended in Marcy projects. Every city I go to, I always want to see what their hood looks like. I didn't actually go in the projects, I stopped at the bodega store across from the projects, to order a cheesesteak. I also like to see if other cities can make cheesesteaks like in Philly.

Outside the projects, right in front of the buildings, was this chubby Spanish guy with no facial hair sitting on the benches. It was obvious he was dealing. He caught my attention because he was screaming, that he was opened for the day. This was different and seemed crazy and dangerous; I was sure he was going to jail. As I sat there and continued to watch him, I became even more amazed.

What blew my mind was when he grabbed this fein off the corner and started talking to him, well, shouting to him. "Yo Unc, come here 'B,' look we getting this thang popping today. You gotta run them in son, every ten you bring me, that's one for you, let's get this mooga." A few minutes later Unc come back with them, one after another. Engulfed in the process so much, I kept count with him. When finally, Unc got to ten, he inquired to the chubby guy "Where's my free one?" The dealer messed up on the count; and insisted that it was only 9 so far and that he owed him one more. Now Unc and the dealer argued, which caused a scene, so I crossed the street and chimed in.

"Who the fuck is you?" fired out of the dealer's mouth. He then clutched at his waistline, as to pull his gun out when he seen me reach my hand in my jacket. He breathed easier once he seen me pull out a $10 bill and hand it to him. "Now it's ten." He stared at me as if I was a cop. I didn't think he even paid attention to things like that, the way he was broadcasting what was going on. To ensure I wasn't a cop, I flashed him my Philadelphia Prison Id, and he just stared at me and then spoke: "Alright pop, what are you doing out here?" I told him I was there to meet some girl, and just stopped to get a bite to eat. He just shook his head up and down. To break the silence,

I asked him. "Yo, what made you pay him to bring you people, I mean, he's just a crackhead right? If he liked your product he was going tell people anyway." He looked at me like I was crazy, and answered "Pap, it don't matter who it is; don't nobody wanna work for free. You feel me B? I give them like a little award for reaching the quota." I shook his hand, turned around to walk back across the street before I was halted in my tracks. **"Yo Pap that's the most important thing you ever going learn, trust me!"** preached the dealer. I continued to the store to get my food and zoned into my thoughts.

Perfect, got it now! When I got back to the city, I jumped right on this new business strategy. Now it was a little different in South Philadelphia because we worked off phones. I started with calling up old customers, asked if they had their fix for the day, and if they didn't, I offered them a proposition. I would pick them up in the car and give them $30 worth- if they took me to a few houses and introduced me. Now this was working, but it was dangerous because if the cops saw us together, we were bound to be pulled over. It also took too much time, so I figured out a smarter alternative. That was, to go over their house and tell them to open their phonebook. Every person they called, if a new customer answered and agreed for me to come over to see them, I would give the old customer a $10 bag. After giving them a $10 a bag, I would have to give the new customer a $10 bag also. This double giving away cost me more but was more effective.

Flip That:

Reward your customers. The most effective marketing to this day is word of mouth. But it's hard to force people to talk about your product- even when they do it's at a slower rate than you would like. To cut down on marketing cost and time, have your customers work for you. Give them free products and discounts and finder's fee for helping you promote your product. This creates ambition in your customers. It also is another way to build brand loyalty **(loyal feins)**, and customer appreciation. It's even better if you can find a way to make a game out of it.

American airlines were the first to use frequent flyer mileage for their company. It was a game created to build brand loyalty. You receive points every time you fly with American Airlines. You get a certain amount of points you get discounts and maybe even a free upgrade on your flight. Also, if you have a certain amount of points you get categorized in different levels. Like gold members, platinum members. This creates a sense of importance and superiority **(power)** within your customers over each other. Then they think, "Why waste a flight with another airline and not get the rewards for it?" Credit unions also use this rewards technique. For example, if you sign up with a credit union because someone referred you, that person will get $50. This effort motivates people to work for you without being an employee.

Branding

"Branding is *one of the most overlooked lessons in life, but it determines if you're first or last on the list, and if you will have one-time buyers or repeat customers.*"

September 2008

`Business was moving fast. I put into play every little lesson learned, although it was a strategic rollercoaster. Now by this time the money was coming in and profits were building and financially, the phone was doing great. The income was up to about $4500 a day. It could have been more, but it was like almost impossible to get to everyone in a timely manner, and at the same time be safe. So, I was okay with it being exactly where it was. All was fine and dandy for the time being, but trying to guarantee the longevity of the business, was a sticky situation. On top of that, my competitiveness kicked in and a new goal surfaced- to stop everyone else from making money. The only way to guarantee business is to brand it. But how do you let people know who you are when the business is a secret.

I got a call one day from my man Flaco. Flaco means skinny in Spanish. He was this Dominican guy from the Bad Lands. Now usually Spanish and blacks have a different swag, but this Dominican guy had the ultimate swag. He was about 6'3, which was rare; he wore every designer clothes out there; he rode in luxury cars, and even rode dirt bikes. He had a bad arm because he got shot in it when somebody tried to rob him, so his bad arm was always in a sling. He made sure that arm stayed with a diamond watch on it though. Flaco owned a dope block on the Northside. Now he had a different type of money. I was doing well, but he was doing excellent.

He wanted me to pull up and smoke some weed with him. I pulled up, parked behind his car and then jumped in the car with him. The blunt was already rolled, so when I got in he just sparked it up. He gave me a nod and a pound. He don't talk much. Whenever we in the car together, he spends most of his time checking his mirrors. I guess after that incident with his arm, he couldn't afford any more surprises.

He asked me how was business. I told him it was good, but there was so much competition; I couldn't figure a way get to the next level, like where I wanted; but it was still good money. He inhaled in let out some smoke. Then he mumbled "Ain't no competition, except yourself." He checked the rearview mirror soon as the last word fell from his lips. Again, he doesn't say much; so, I had to pull this wisdom out of him. "What's that supposed to mean?" I questioned. He shot back with "50 dope blocks down here, I'm still rich; figure it out." That statement started the war. Defensively, I returned fire with "It ain't much more to do; my bag is bigger, my product is better, and I'm 24/7." He looked at me, took another pull on the blunt and said, "That's physical, use your brain; brand it."

"How the hell you brand drugs, you sound crazy." I laughed. He pulled a bag of dope out of his pocket. Now on Heroin bags, people put stamped names on it, so the customer can know what dope it is; they need it to be good every time.

Every block uses their own name or symbol. Usually it's a name like killer, die hard, dope dick, or some picture of a person that's been in the media a lot lately. But this bag had a stop sign on it, and I was lost. In my head I asked, Why a stop sign? What is the catchy part to this stop sign?" He eyeballed me, blew the remainder smoke out his mouth, and passed me the blunt and whispered, "It tripled my cash flow."

He could tell I was still lost; so, for once he continued his speech. "How do people get to my block?" He fell silent. I guess that was my cue to answer. "They walk, or they drive." I answered the question like it was stupid. But at the same time, I was waiting for the bombshell. He was going to pull some words out of that brain of his if he expected me to get it. "A Stop sign is on every corner, so while they're driving, walking, thinking about who block to buy their fix from, they constantly see my symbol. It's like me having a free billboard on every corner. So subconsciously, they're being guided to my block." He ended the conversation with **"Best lesson you'll ever learn."**

A lost for words I just hit the blunt. I was in all, first by the theory of this symbol but second by the fact that I never heard Flaco use more than five words at a time- not to mention his vocabulary wasn't that bad.

Flip That:

When you market your product, it doesn't always have to be dead on. You can build a link to another product that's totally unrelated. If done right, it can force a reminder in your customers that they never even knew.

For instance, the Fiat car is linked to the blue pill which resembles Viagra. The commercial starts with an older guy popping open the pill before having sex. He drops the pill out the window. It rolls throughout the street until it hits a bump and lands in the gas tank of a Fiat. The car gets bigger and more muscular. The car is now the Fiat 500. The correlation (link) is, Viagra makes its customer bigger and stronger and the Fiat 500 is now bigger and stronger from taking it.

Now every time someone sees a Viagra pill they will remember that commercial. They will think Fiat when they see Viagra and vice versa. So, both companies double their marketing by joining forces, every time Viagra spends x amount of dollars on posters and commercials, it's like Fiat did also and vice versa.

An even better example is the Tabaco company. The Tabaco Company invest in anti-smoking commercials. You see the more they can get people to listen too, read about and remember smoking the better. It doesn't matter that the advertisement is stop smoking, because sub consciously all people hear is smoke.

DARKNESS TO LIGHT: HOW TO LEARN ENTREPRENEURSHIP FROM A RETIRED DRUG DEALER

Insurance

"This is the underdog of business. The most looked over expense, that's actually your life saver."

Oct 2008

On Halloween night, my dad and I decided to go get a drink. You see, my dad ain't your average dad. He a young man just in an older body. Being out with him is like being out with one of my friends. We were out drinking and having fun that eventually turned into a pissing match. The test was to see who could take the most shots? Who could get the most numbers? But it was all just fun and games. When it was time to leave, we staggered out the door like two frat boys on thirsty Thursday.

We walked to the car and was surprised by a masked man who jumped out from an alley; his arms were raised in a grabbing motion. Startled, I stepped back, but my dad lunged forward, punched the guy in the face and then wrestled him to the ground. The guy frantically yelled: "It's a prank! It's a prank!" That confession stopped my dad from executing another blow to his face. In a hurry, he snatched his mask off, revealing a puddle of red blood where his nose used to be. Once I seen the new paint job on his face, I stepped in to help the guy up, and patted him on the back; "I apologized for my father's action" I pleaded. When the guy ran off, I looked over to my dad, and we burst into laughter. We kept laughing the whole stroll to the car.

We headed home. We were caught at a red light, when my dad looked around; to admire the car I just bought. "Nice whip son. This a man's car right here. You never go wrong with a Cadillac or black leather," he praised. "Thanks, yeah, I thought of you when I bought this." I lied. "Solid, I see you always trying to steal my swag." he snickered, and added, "I can't even tell where the stash spot is in this jawn." I ignored his remark because I didn't have a stash, but I know I needed one.

We pulled up in front of his house, he turned to me before getting out, and baited me with "I had a good time son; I'm just glad you ain't pull out your pistol when the guy jumped out at us, because that would have ended badly." Then he laughed to himself. At this point I know he is fishing for information from me- basically, just checking to see if I'm on my toes. I got out in front of it, "Pop, I don't carry a gun. I mean, that's an extra 5 years if you get caught with gun and drugs." He slammed the door, took a deep breath before the words crept out of his mouth, "Son, if you out here selling drugs without a gun, you are hustling backwards. The stick-up boys will sit around and wait for you to make all your money and then take it. Then you're back to square one." He tapped my chest and told me to tighten up. He turned to leave the car, closed the door behind him then turned back towards the car. He motioned for me to roll the window down. When I did he leaned his forearm where the window would be and told me **"Son, nobody in this game, will ever tell you anything more important than that."** He tapped the roof of the car and proceeded to his front door.

Flip That:

Now this scenario may be a little a confusing, but it is vital. It has nothing to do with making money or gaining business but with protecting what you have. You see, marketing, sales and distribution is all great, but it doesn't mean anything if your paperwork ain't right. The major part of business that people miss is the business part. You must make sure everything is covered before you create a business. Make sure you have your licenses, permits and most importantly, your insurances and taxes. Otherwise, you can make all the money you want, but in an instant, one mess up will take all that from you.

I did some volunteer work down at a homeless shelter one time. This one guy, Tracy, stood out too me. When we started talking, he let me know that he used to be a millionaire. He went through a divorce over his alcohol problem. In the settlement, he gave his wife all the properties and the savings and he kept the construction business. It was a 1.4 million dollar a year company, so he was fine with it. He was sleeping in his office until he found another place.

During the divorce procedure, he became depressed and started to drink even more. This started to affect his business, his friendships and worst his sense of responsibility. He was months behind on every bill and had bills and mail piled up on his desk. He left in the middle of the night one night to run to deli and get some beer. He fell asleep in the car on some back-block drunk.

When he returned to his business, it was totally burned down and taped off. When he checked his phone, he had over a hundred missed calls and messages informing him of what was happening. When he left he knocked his space heater over and it caused a fire. Everything would have been okay except he didn't pay his insurance bill. So they dropped him to make things worst most of the equipment in the warehouse was on lease. He now owed over a million dollars and had no home, no money and no business.

Now obviously there were way more problems going on with this guy but if he had insurance he could have at least maintained an income. A few months later, the taskforce did a sting operation and I was arrested in the middle of it. Since I was on probation, there was no bail and no pass to go just straight to jail.

Who Got My Money
~Grant Cardone

This rule drastically increased my cash flow, which in turn fattened my pockets. This is what separated the boys from the men, the lightweights from the heavyweights, the 4 ½ coppers from the eight ball coppers.

February 2009

I had just gotten released from prison for the second time. I sat for only about 3 months until all charges were dismissed. 3 weeks into being home, I was ready to start making money again because, since being home I spent more than expected. My stash of money wasn't too bad; a few thousands were saved, and one of my friends gave me a cut of the money he made when he took care of the phone business while I was away, so that added a few more thousand. I wanted to hold onto this as long as possible.

I beat my case; and even though I prayed and pleaded with God that if I won this case, I would never return to the game, nevertheless, I did. I had just spent a few months building my first successful street phone business, and I just couldn't let it go to waste. The only problem was, what I built was only meant for one person, so with two people now, since my friend stayed on, income was average. So, I just walked away from it.

Crack cocaine was scary to me now anyway. After hearing all the stories in prison of people getting sentenced to 5 and 10 years for dealing it, I didn't want to chance it. But what really impacted me was my cellmate Josh. He was this red head Irish kid with blue eyes and only two fingers on his right hand; his index and thumb. He still had a habit of talking with his hands, so whenever he was talking to you it always looked like he was point a gun at you.

Many nights we stayed up late and talked and reminisced about our nights of freedom in the streets. This one night. He broke down and cried to me about how he had lost everything he had to crack cocaine. His wife left him, he lost his million-dollar landscaping business and his mother passed away while he was in rehab. He told me "Stay away from selling products that cause harm to others bro. There is no good that can come of it. Stick to party and fun drugs, where people aren't selling their souls just to get high." That advice replayed in my mind for months while being home, so I decided to go back to my college days. Powder seem to be a lot less detrimental and it carried less time.

Now in the city, I was totally clueless with the ins and outs of the cocaine business. But I used my tactics and figured it out. Few weeks in business started to pick up and I was making a consistent cash flow. I was on the overnight shift working the phone when things got kind of slow. I stopped in a local old folks' bar because it's usually drama free; most of them are all bark and no bite and when some biting does occur, it's just a flesh wound. The plan was to drink a shot and then take it in for the night.

As I entered the bar, it greeted me with the smells of stale perfume and cigarette smoke, and the sounds of Marvin Gay blasting out of the juke box. I spotted one of my closest friends at the time, Birdman. He was feeling it. I know he was a little more than tipsy because he was treating the whole bar to shots, and tipped the bartender with twenties, and when I asked him "You know you're throwing twenties at the bartender right?" He replied, "I threw a couple of them." Funny as it was, after that remark, I figured he had enough and convinced him to let me drive him home, and he agreed.

When we pulled up in front of his house, I just had to jump on his case "Why every night you're at the bar drinking and carrying on when we supposed to be getting this money?" He turns to me in a drunken slur and says "Boy, that's what I'm doing here; everybody who snorts this powder also drinks in the bars. The powder keeps them up, so they can drink more. So, I party with them. **That's the number one rule Anthony!**" He always called me by my middle name when he was teaching me a lesson. I thought he was drunk, so I paid him no mind.

The next morning, I had a delivery to make. When I rang the bell, I expected Bobby or one of his old friends to answer the door but to my surprise a young black kid came to the door. Not just any kid, it was "Biggs," one of the legends. Never understood why that was his name because he was skinny; but every dealer who was somebody knew who this guy was. He had been around for a long time and been making money for years. He invited me in and called Bobby downstairs. He gave bobby a high five and continued to stand there rolling up his weed.

After Bobby and I made the transaction, I rushed to my car, pulled out my good phone and called my guy. Slim answered the phone after the third ring. The moment he picked up the phone my lips began playing the tune. Gossiping about what I had seen; I stumbled over my words trying to tell him what I thought was going to be ground breaking news. "Slim, I think Biggs, is getting high. He is sitting in Bobby's house, relaxing and smoking weed." Slim just laughed and laughed and laughed. When he finally got himself together, he fixed my confusion, "Naw AHK, you read that wrong. That's what he does; he hangs around them all day, eats with them, party with them, and even tricks with them, all so they will always cop off him.

How you think he became "a legend"?"

Then I thought about it. That's what Birdman was saying! After that, I found myself hanging out at all the college parties in the nearby area. I met friends in the local pizza shop near the major universities and got the leads on all the frat parties. In just a few weeks my sales grew from a $500 a day, to almost $1500.

Flip That:

In business, you want to surround yourself with those who want what you are selling. There is no point of wasting time being around people who don't want, don't need or have any interest in your product. If you want to always be selling, and always making money, then find out who got your money and be engulfed with them. That's how you keep an unlimited supply of customers.

For example, if you are a personal trainer then your days should be spent in a gym. Why? Because that's where your customers are. If you are constantly around your fat friends who eat what they want and sit around all day, preaching to them about getting in shape and hiring you is a waste of time. You want to be around those who already have an interest in your service. Those who already took some initiative in finding, what you have to offer.

2009-2010

Now selling powder is safer and less harmful, but it still has its cons. The biggest con is that the people you deal with are from suburban backgrounds, so they don't follow the "no telling rule." One day a real popular defense attorney got pulled over and busted for dui. While his car was searched for any open bottles, the police found a small bag of cocaine. They instantly threatened his license and career unless he told where he

got his drugs from. He turned me in, and was set up, and within a few months was incarcerated again. This time I wasn't so lucky because of the status of the victim, there was no getting out of this. I did about a year in prison, and then released to the streets again.

While waiting about an hour in the bubble, which is a room where everybody on their way out of prison must stay in until their turn to leave; this Caucasian guy was talking to someone about why he was arrested. His story instantly caught my attention. First, he was in prison for burning his own house down. But what spiked my interest was the articulate way he talked. Anyone could tell he wasn't your typical criminal, but he had a certain calm to him like this wasn't his first rodeo. I chimed into the conversation and asked if he played a sport. I just threw that out there because he was about 6'2 and athletically built with a jogging sweat suit on. On your way out of prison, you wear whatever you were arrested in. He bit the bait and told me about his baseball career in college.

That opened the door for more of my questions, "If you were in college, why would you be here?" That's when he went on to tell me that he burned his house down because his wife allowed his teenage daughter's boyfriend to live there, without asking his permission. As the days went on he was pushed further outside their circle and the boyfriend was being accepted more.

One day he came home from working and seen that the boy had his robe on, so he snapped.

He asked me what I was in here for. I began to tell him but couldn't finish because he just laughed in the middle of the explanation. He interrupted me with "I ruined my whole life putting that stuff up my nose. I was a successful investment banker until I got addicted to that. Look, I ain't telling you how to live your life, but if you're going back to that life, don't sell a drug that destroy lives. Just mess with a drug that's as harmless as possible- if they exist."

Different Fish, Same Stream

"The fastest, simplest and most straightforward path to becoming financially independent"

April 2010

This year wasn't that good for me. I wasn't broke, but I wasn't balling either. After that last bid, I was a little shaken up; So, I switched to marijuana. It was a lighter sentence and less traffic, but that equals less money. Now I was getting by and could profit about two hundred dollars a day which is way better than a job, but it wasn't powder money, and defiantly was crack money. It was time for me to add another stream of income.

On Thursday morning of every week, the PPA (Philadelphia Parking Authority) held an auction. That's where they auction off all the cars that get booted. Oftentimes, if people couldn't pay their tickets, they would lose their cars. Many cars came from live stops. Now the live stopped cars were the goldmine, it was usually a car of a drug dealer, that didn't have insurance or a license.

Auction day came around. I went, stood in line, got my number and starting bidding. I won three cars, all Cadillacs. My father's words about a Cadillac rang in my ears. You can never go wrong with a Cadillac in the hood. After taking care of everything with registration and checking them out with the mechanics; they were ready to sell. One sold in a matter of weeks, not too bad and I even made a pretty penny. The other two took a few more weeks after that but still no loss and a nice profit on them. But I never returned to the auction again. What I underestimated was the time it took to actually market and successfully sell a car. And time, was money.

The value of time, became clearer to me once I ran into, "Smoke". Smoke was my wealthiest, as far as street money goes, pot head clients. Now Smoke was a major player in the coke game. Whenever he called me, he always bought everything I had. I had a few others on my list like him who called me, but Smoke was like family. His phone calls were priority to me.

I pulled up on the corner he was standing on, he jumped in the car, clean as always. Fresh haircut, even though his hairline started in the middle of his head he would still get it shaped up. He wore a versatile sweat suit, Gucci sneakers and a plane Jane Rolex **(no diamonds).** His first words to me were, "I'm hearing your name all through the grapevine." My eyes lit up with pride until he deflated my ego, "You falling off. Everybody's talking about how you ain't showing up and how taking long as shit to get to the traps; Wassup with you?"

I stared at him in deep thought before any word escaped my mouth; and exhaled "It's these cars man; I didn't realize it was that noticeable, but I needed another income because this weed is a little slower than I'm used to. But every time somebody calls to check out a car, I miss my traps. They wanna ask questions, and take test drives, and all that just takes up all the time. Then on the other hand, if I'm running around making money, then I'm missing the people who want to check out a car. I don't know what to do, man." I put my head into my prayer hands in frustration. I peeked up and saw Smoke just staring at me; and once we made eye contact, he just chuckled. He motioned for me to come a little closer. He looked both ways to make sure no one was listening to him. He leaned towards my ear and murmured **"Nephew, what I'm bout to tell you will be the best and only advice you ever going need, to be rich"** he continued. "You see, the problem is that you already mastered the stream, but you're trying to find a way to swim in the Ocean. If you want more income or multiple streams of income, then just piggy back off what's already working. Figure out what else your clientele uses besides weed. Most people who smoke weed take pills, sip syrup, or hell, maybe they just need wrapping papers. Get different fish but use the same stream!"

FLIP THAT:

In business, it's always great to have multiple streams of income; this way if one field hits a rough patch, you can always make money. Most millionaires in the world have more than one income. But what's even more important than multiple streams of income, is having them all working together; this way, there's less resources used. It's great if you already have a pre-clientele base, then not as much time and effort is taken away from the original source. The moral of the story is: to make more money by finding more streams of income. But find a way to make money within your business, and not around it.

For instance, if you sell used cars, then also be certified to register them. If you cut hair or do hair, then make your own hair products and sell them in your salon or shop. If you have a nice food restaurant that people enjoy eating from, then offer cooking classes or better yet write a cook book and sell those.

Entrepreneur

"Without the proper use of leverage, to making you money. You can never call yourself this."

August 2010

Coming over the Ben Franklin Bridge into the city- after taking this 2-hour ride from New York, I got pulled over. Now my heart was somewhere between my back pockets and the seat belt. Supposedly I was speeding, but who knows with Philly cops. I was pulled out of my car while it was searched, but thankfully this time nothing was found. But that was all I needed....... another sign from God that I refused to ignore. It was time to sit down for a while. I went home, rolled me up a blunt and knocked on Ahkmed's door. In only a few years, everything about him had changed. The bald spot that used to be in the middle of his head had gradually turned into a full fledge bald head, but it looked good on him. His beard went from a few strands of gray to a full face of gray hair; and he walked and talked a little slower. But his mind was still sharp. He came outside and hit the blunt with me. And he listened to me vent about all my jail sentences and problems.

After I was finished talking, he took a while to respond. I figured he was taking it all in or just trying to see if I would start talking again. I did a few times, but eventually I was totally quiet. In between inhales he took his time to tell me "Your biggest problem is that you don't know when enough is enough. It's time for you to become an entrepreneur." Then he exhaled. So as usual, when he talks I get defensive because, I don't know, in some way I know he's write but I can't make it that easy for him. So, I countered, "I am an entrepreneur. I don't work for anybody and I always make my own money when I get out of jail." He shook his head and asked me a question, "Do you think a barber is an entrepreneur or self-employed? I know you want to say entrepreneur as most people do, youngan! But you see; a barber is self-employed, until he puts more chairs in his barbershop and rents them out to other barbers. Then he becomes an entrepreneur.

If you must work to make money, then you're just self-employed. Figure out how to make your money without taking that risk. **That's the number one lesson of business, son**." When he was finished talking he just passed the blunt and then turned around and walked back up the stairs. I guess he was tired.

As usual I took his advice to heart and I ran with it. I began recruiting people with a license and a car, especially those who needed a job. I preferred women because it was less of a chance they would get pulled over, but most of time the job was too much for them to want to deal with. I gave everyone certain hours to work and paid them a certain amount every day. Now, although I was paying money out; I was making more money because once people knew we were open 24 hours, it was nonstop business. Few weeks go by and the money I should be making I'm not. I mean, I know how much I would sell in 8 hours; with 24 hours to work with, it would be triple, but it wasn't. It was only about a little less than double.

On my way to get a hot sausage from the cart at the shopping plaza, Smoke pulled up next to me in his jeep. He rolled his window down, arm hanging out the window "Oh, you a big shot now, huh Neph? You don't even meet people no more." I laughed "Naw, it ain't like that; just trying to free up some time for the family." "Yeah, I can dig that, but is it financially beneficial?" I responded "A little bit more. I thought it was going be better." He flew right into preacher mode with "Well, you would make more money if they actually answered the phone when we called." I could feel the temperature of my face heating up. To stay calm, I shook my head and vented out "I don't understand these guys Smoke; I pay them 100 dollars every day to do a job, and they just do what they want anyway." Smoke lowered his glasses from his eyes to the brim of his nose. Cold giveaway of a lesson coming on. He put his hazards lights on to signal the cars to go around while he began class. Then he started "Well, Neph. That's your problem right there. They don't have to work hard; you going to pay them anyway. They get paid regardless of their work ethic. If they work hard they get $100. If they bullshit they get $100. So why wouldn't they just put in less work and still get paid?"

I looked down at my lap as to see the money sitting there, and then looked back up to him and inquired "How do I fix that?" The glasses came off the face this time. "You should really try sharing your profits with them, this way they only get paid based on how much they move. This way you won't be paying a $100 for $50 worth of work. But then if they know they can make more, they might work harder. **That's the number one rule Neph.** Get it together." He turned his music up and pulled off.

Flip That:

If the only way you make money is through your own labor, then you're self-employed. Now this is much better then working for someone else; but it is not the Ultimate goal. Being self-employed puts a limit to your growth and stops expandability- thereby putting a ceiling on the business and profits. You want to create a business with a system that can run on autopilot. That does not mean you should not be a part of the running of the company, but you should not have to handle every task. You want to be able to make money when you're not around.

For example, McDonald's got started with only one restaurant. They were doing good business with just the one location. But it didn't become the fast-food giant it is today until it started to sell franchises. This allowed them to be in many places at one time, and it allowed the CEO to make money off the backs of others. The corporation started making money by supplying all the franchisees with the McDonald's products. Then eventually, it moved into its largest money maker, real-estate. To this day McDonalds' largest income comes from its real estate holdings, and not its food. The other lesson is that people work harder for you when they feel they benefit or lose from the ups and downs of the company. So, by sharing profits or giving them stocks in your company, the employees feel a bigger sense of responsibility and importance, which in return causes them to put forth stronger and more efficient efforts.

The Market Talks, You Don't

"Unless you have figured out the next best thing or the solution to the world's largest problem then this is the only way you will survive."

April 2011

Six months has passed now, and everything is running smoothly. With all the free time from not having to do the day- to-day work; I was able to enroll back into college. My savings were used to buy me a house from the sheriff's auction. The majority of the money was spent on fixing it up. I figured that was okay because at least I'll own something, and eventually I'll get that money back.

Two weeks after the house was fully finished, my assets included: a brand-new house, about $2000 in cash, and $4000 in product and 2 cars. So now it was time to save back up. The evening of the first night of me sleeping in my new home, I received a call in the middle of the night from one of the workers on the phone. The task force had just raided the stash house, but he was able to sneak out the back window. A stash house was a house that was in an anonymous person's name; it was like a headquarters. It was where the product was bagged, weighed and distributed. The stash house was also used as a place to chill and bring girls- to party with.

The story involved one of the workers, whose whole life revolved around sleeping with as many women as he could. He was in the house with one girl while another girl caught him; and they begin to argue. Out of spite, she called the cops and told them everything. They raided the house and locked up everyone, except the one that escaped, and the one person that was running around on the phone at the time. They found all the product because we had just started getting it together.

I spent whatever money I had received from the workers and the money in my stash to pay all the bails. At that point, I was stuck with a business with no product to sell, no money to buy more, and no house to store it in. I bowed out, and decided to just get a job, save up more money and head back to school in the first semester in September. Work was hard to get, but eventually I landed a job at a small cleaning company. Slaving hard all summer for $8 an hour only got me $1500 in savings by August 1st. That wasn't even enough to start school with; it barley was even enough to start a payment plan.

It's been months since the phone has been up and running and there was very little time to start it back up. I needed money bad and a job wasn't going cut it if I planned on getting back into school. After days of thinking it over, I made a call to my friend J-rock. J-rock, was this guy I happen to meet in prison when I was arrested out the county. He was from Philly, but he traveled to different small towns to make his money. He was making a killing out in Stroudsburg. It was a small town about 3 hours away from the city. Ten-dollar bags of heroin were going for $25, and $10 bags of crack and powder cocaine was going for $20 a bag.

When I talk to J-rock and told him my plan was to come out there with weed and sell to all the drug dealers. I could sell my $10 bags for $20. He gave me some advice, like what type of cars to drive, what areas to avoid and hangout spots where all the dealers hung out. When the weekend came around, I took my savings and bought as much product as I could; I rented a car and drove out there. My plan proved to be a failure. From Friday to Sunday, I made only $150. It seemed like everybody in Stroudsburg was hooked on opiates, even the dealers. I couldn't believe it; I'm in a city where most dealers get rich, and I can't even make a few pennies.

My dad called my phone to check to see how the job was treating me. I let him in on my new venture that was flopping. He kept quiet and allowed me to get it all out. Most of the conversation was self-sabotaging. When I finally stopped talking, my dad jumped in. He proclaimed, "Now that you're finished grinding yourself up son, you made the mistake that every rookie dealer makes, and you ain't even a rookie. When you go O.T. (outta town) or even in your own city, you gotta sell the drug that everybody wants. Nobody cares that you got weed; if they don't want weed, you're wasting your time. That's a heroin city; sell some heroin."

I reacted, "I'm not selling that stuff. First, I don't want to take that type of risk. Plus, my karma is already messed up; there's no need to add more strikes against it." He simplified it for me "Well, go home then. Point blank." **"And son ain't nobody going tell you nothing better than that. Best advice I can ever give you."**

Flip That:

When creating a business, most new business owners have the habit of creating a business around what they want to do, which is backwards. The best chance you have at being profitable is by researching the market first. Find out what people want or what people are missing, then supply that. Create a service or product according to what your customers are willing to spend their money on. Create something that will provide value to your community; and the money will follow. Don't create a business based on your emotional attachment to that service or product. If you choose to create a business from what you want, then you need to relocate to the area that wants your business. Anything else is a waste of time and money.

Just imagine a butcher whose specialty is roasted pork; and he moves to an Islamic community to sell his product. He spends all his money to open a restaurant, displaying a picture of a pig on the store front; and his whole menu is pig feet, pork chops and chitterlings. This would be the worst thing he could ever try to sell to a Muslim; they would be offended. Not only would he not make money; he would probably earn a bad name and reputation and would perhaps never be able to sell any products in that area again. The advice is to know your market!

September 2011

When I came back from the weekend vacation, reality set in. The time for school was around the corner; bills were due, and my refrigerator was empty. The job was still available to me because I took a little vacation, to try my hand out of town first. The plan was to switch my schedule to weekends and go to school during the week; but that never happened because my dream of going back to school was instantly a fantasy without a way to pay for it.

Marijuana was the only logical solution at that time. It was the only way to temporarily drain the pain. While walking to the store to get a Backwood, a young guy from the block, started to walk with me and talk to me. He was crying the blues about how he was badly in need of product- before he loses all his business. He claimed his supplier was arrested and now he was stuck with a business and no product. I laughed. This story was all too familiar. We walked back from the store with a Backwood; a bottle of water; a bag of chips, and some seeds. The young guy was still rambling, but I was in a different space at the time.

We sat on the steps; we smoked and talked. He bragged about all the money he made; and I just tried to warn him of all the bad that could come from it. In the middle of the smoke session I realized that I could probably use this young guy to get my money back. I passed him the blunt and asked him if he liked that weed? He coughed uncontrollably, and then answered with a "This is some gas; if I had this I'd be back, real rap." I smiled, those were the exact words I needed to hear.

I ran into the house and came back out with two sandwich bags full of weed, which was equal to $600. His eyes lit up. After agreeing to my price and time range, he snatched it out of my hand and ran down the street to get to work. If everything worked out, I would stand to make $2400, which would at least get me my money back and a nice profit.

A few days later, and on schedule, he knocked on my door and handed me my money. This time gave him the entire amount of weed I had. There was no reason for me to sit on it. We discussed the new time frame for this package and shook hands on it. My job was to just sit back and wait. Two days after the scheduled time, I still hadn't heard from him. I called his phone and walked through his block, but he was nowhere to be found. About a week after, I had to face the fact, it was obvious that he ran away with the money and product.

Few more days later, a phone call came through, that he was staying out West Philly with his cousin. My first reaction was to go around to my grandfather's house. I know what you are thinking, but trust me, just like I said about my dad, my grandfather ain't your typical grandfather. He was a business man and an old gangsta. He had three wives and one of them was my age. His youngest son was six years old and he had a few around my age, and one who at the time was 17 and he was like my best friend. My grandfather drove a new Cadillac and played Jay-z all day long in his car. He demanded respect everywhere he went and still to this day he loves drama.

I knocked on the door for a while; he eventually opened the door and let me in. My grandfather stood 6'3 inches tall with not a strand of gray hair on his head. He walked and talked as if he was my dad age and ain't miss a step. He saw the distress on my face and stared in my eyes. He just waited for me to tell him what was wrong. I told him I needed to hold his gun; I had to take care of something. His face told it all. He asked no questions. He escalated up the stairs, five minutes later he appeared downstairs dressed in all black; two guns in hand and two ski masks in his back pockets.

I opened the door to leave out and my grandfather slammed it closed. He took a deep breathe to calm himself down leaning on the door, he starred at the floor and asked me what happened. I told him the story. He looked up at me with a softer face and a sort of smirk as if he was holding his laughter in. Then he snatched the gun back from me. "Sit down, dummy!" he demanded. I did what he told me and watched him run up the steps. He strolled back down with his ball shorts and t-shirt that he had on earlier, with one addition, a blunt.

He went into speech mode, "Ibn (son in Arabic), first off, that ain't enough money to be risking your freedom over. Second, that's your fault. Why would you give him everything? You never give somebody credit if you can't handle the loss. Never put your whole livelihood into somebody else's hands based on their words. You f*** that money up!" Then he took a puff of the blunt and continued "Ibn please listen to what I'm telling you. **That advice will save your life**. Don't nobody love you I love. **And ain't nobody going tell you that such good advice for nothing, you hear me**."

Flip That:

In business, never allow your accounts receivable to dictate the outcome of your business. In other words, never give consignment to a person unless you know they have the clientele to handle it. And even if they can handle it, never give them so much that if for some unforeseen incident occur and they lose it all, it won't affect your ability to get back. Set aside a certain amount of product that you can afford to lose. Also, if you're going to do services or products for payments later, run a credit check. Make the person have some skin in the game. Put up some type of money or collateral up. If they want $2000 on credit, make them put up $500 or an item that's work at least $1000 on resell.

Let's break it down in math. If you buy a product for a $1000, and if you sell it yourself you can make $1600. Then that means you can only afford to give $600 out on credit without risking a loss. And if you smart you will only give out $300, giving yourself an option to still make $300 profit.

Abu, my grandfather in Arabic, passed me the blunt that was lit. He turned back around to go up his stairs; he left me there in deep thought. I tilted my head back and just stared at the ceiling reminiscing about how my life turned out. Thinking what it would have been like if I just lived right in the beginning. But then I thought about what I could do from that moment on- to change to a better path. Pictures of every story, every mistake, and every lesson I ever learned played like a long college class in my mind.

Trying to figure out what it all meant, I left my Abu's house and headed home. When I walked onto my street, headed up my steps, and reached my front door, I dug into my pocket to get the keys; I got snatched by a man dressed in all black. I started to try to fight back until I heard the dreadful words "Freeze, this is the police!" I whipped around, and saw the young guy sitting there, smiling. It was all a set up. After the stash house got raided, my own folks turned me in. The cops set up a sting, and I fell for it. They had watched me for a few months; and were going to let me go due to lack of evidence, until my greed drove me back in the game.

Now with my record, jay walking would get me two years in prison. While I sat in the back of the police car, head launched back on the headrest. Right then and there I vowed that no matter what happened, I was finished with the streets.

The judge sentenced me to exactly what I thought: 2 to 4 years. This time was going to be different. No wasted hours on the phone. No fiction novels meant to help me forget where I was. It was time for growth. Time for change. Time to reshape my body and my mind. Vegetarian diet, Consistent work outs and daily practice of yoga and meditation. Only read literature that taught me mind control and useful skill. I worked on my body and health, and even became a vegan not so much for health reasons, but because I was afraid of the karma. It turned out that most of the reason I sold drugs was because my ego controlled my thinking; it never allowed my true self to shine through. Who knew? Three years later, I was released to society and was forced to figure out a new way of life.

I jotted down all the lessons I ever learned on a napkin. No order just how I remembered them. Figured I start with my past up until the present. Only way for these lessons to stay imprinted in my heart was to write about them. So, I wrote. I just started writing about the first lesson of business I learned while in college. That lesson was: "See what people already like and start there."

These lessons, where the most important lessons of my life.

MIKE KIETT

Made in the USA
San Bernardino, CA
17 February 2020